# Warning!
# No One Is Scared Of Hell
# Until They Get There:
# I Have Been There

# Warning!
# No One Is Scared of Hell Until They Get There:
# I Have Been There

Lannie Richmond

Fresh Ink Group
Roanoke

# Warning!
# No One Is Scared of Hell
# Until They Get There:
# I Have Been There

Copyright © 2014
by Lannie Richmond
All rights reserved

Fresh Ink Group
An Imprint of:
The Fresh Ink Group, LLC
PO Box 525
Roanoke, TX 76262
Email: info@FreshInkGroup.com
www.FreshInkGroup.com

| Edition 1.0 | 2013 |
| Version 1.1 | 2014 |

Book design by Ann Stewart
Cover design by Muhammad Anwar Manzoor

Scripture quotations marked NIV are from the Holy Bible New International Version © 1973, 1978, 1984, 2011 by Biblica, Inc. Used by permission. All rights reserved.

Scripture quotations marked NJKV are from the Holy Bible, New King James Version Copyright © 1982 by Thomas Nelson, Inc.

Scripture quotations marked KJV are from the King James Version of the Bible.

Scripture quotations marked NLT are from the Holy Bible, New Living Translation, Copyright © 1996, 2004, 2007 by Tyndale House Foundation. Used by permission of Tyndale House Publishers, Inc., Carol Stream Illinois 60188. All rights reserved.

Some names of persons mentioned in this book have been changed to protect privacy; any similarity between individuals described in this book to individuals known to readers is purely coincidental.

Except as permitted under the U.S. Copyright Act of 1976, no part of this publication may be reproduced, distributed, or transmitted in any form or by any means, or stored in a database or retrieval system, without prior written permission of the publisher.

Cataloging-in-Publication Recommendations: Religion;
Religion/Christian; Religion/Protestant; Spirituality

Library of Congress Control Number: 2014932657
ISBN-13: 978-1-936442-19-5

# Dedication

To my wife Lori who is a woman that is a great encourager to me.

My three children Penny Van Mourik, David, and Michael Richmond.

My five grandchildren who bring me great joy: Brianna, Brook, and Brock Van Mourik; David Jr. and Caleb Richmond.

# Acknowledgements

We acknowledge our Lord and only Savior of the Whole World, Jesus Christ. He is the way, the truth, and the life. We thank Him for His death on the cross and resurrection. He is the only hope for the whole world.

# Table of Contents

| | | |
|---|---|---|
| Chapter 1 | My Life | 1 |
| Chapter 2 | Satan and Demons | 7 |
| Chapter 3 | Satan's Lies | 13 |
| Chapter 4 | My Experience in Hell | 22 |
| Chapter 5 | The Soul, the Real Life of Man | 27 |
| Chapter 6 | People | 35 |
| Chapter 7 | Jesus | 41 |
| Chapter 8 | Born Again (Saved) | 47 |
| Chapter 9 | Deceiving Sins | 51 |
| Chapter 10 | Love | 59 |

# Chapter 1
## My Life

I went to church as a young child. I thought that simply being good was the way to heaven. When I was fourteen years old, my uncle Ollie Davis lead me to Jesus. I thank God he took the time and talked to me about Jesus. I was sincere and asked Jesus to come into my heart and life. Jesus showed me the power of the Holy Spirit. I felt the joy and peace only Jesus gives.

> *I pray that God, the source of hope, will fill you completely with joy and peace because you trust in him. Then you will overflow with confident hope through the power of the Holy Spirit.*
>
> —ROMANS 15:13 (NLT)

After I accepted Jesus, people saw a big change in me. I no longer wanted to sin, and no longer enjoyed sinning. I was a new person born again from above. I told God I would never go back to a life of sin.

Unfortunately, I began to let the pressures of life and harassment from students and teachers at school shake my resolve. I started to let my feelings control me, and after just six months, I turned my back on God. I went back to my old sinful ways. I made a big mistake when I followed my feelings about my salvation through Christ, because being saved has nothing to do with any feeling. Don't go by your feelings. *Salvation has nothing to do with how you feel.*

## A Second Chance

At twenty-three, God's Holy Spirit led me back to God, and I repented.

I asked God to forgive me, and I started over again with God.

I told God I would never backslide on him again. You are saved by God's grace—a free gift.

> *God saved you by his grace when you believed. And you can't take credit for this; it is a gift from God. Salvation is not a reward for the good things we have done, so none of us can boast about it.*
>
> *—EPHESIANS 2:8-9 (NLT)*

After two years I had a new house built, which was about twenty miles away from my church. I would say, "I'm not going to church this Sunday; instead I will go next Sunday."

But when the next Sunday came, I again said the same thing. "I'm not going to church this Sunday. I will go next Sunday." After time, I had no interest in God or in church. I went back to a life of sin again. When you and I live in sin, the devil—our enemy—moves in on us. My disobedience opened a door for the devil, and my wife divorced me. We had one child together.

One night I had a dream, and it was real. I was sleeping in my bedroom in the house I grew up in. There was a ceiling light in the house, and I went to turn it on. It came on really bright, then flickered, and then went into really black darkness. It was scary. I jumped up and turned the light on for a second time. It came on really bright, flickered again, and went back again to that deep darkness.

I woke up and I wondered what the dream meant. I told it to my uncle, who explained to me that it represented my life. The bright light represented the time in my life when I was serving Christ. The flickering represented my falling away; and the darkness, my living in sin. When I backslid the second time, I experienced a physical death, and I went to hell. I will tell about this experience in Chapter 4.

If God has spoken a promise to you, remember if we are faithful to God he will be faithful to his words spoken to us. God's timing is always on his timetable, not ours. God is never late. Maybe He is still working on you. God called Moses the great leader of Israel when Moses was eighty years old. God is in control.

I came back to God again when I was thirty-four. I was divorced and single, and had been for eight years. I started to pray and ask God for a Christian wife. God spoke to me and said, "Be patient." I knew He had someone for me. God is a good God and He loves us. I met my wife Lori on a Tuesday, and three days later we were engaged to be married. Three months after our engagement, we were married. It was June 19, 1982.

My wife and I have been married over thirty years now, and we have two boys, David and Michael. David has two boys, seven-year-old David Jr., whom I nicknamed DJ, and four-year-old Caleb. My wife Lori is the godliest women I have ever met. God has spoken to Lori and me about a worldwide ministry calling on our life.

# Chapter 2
# Satan and Demons

Satan is a master at deceiving people, and he is all evil. There is no love, kindness, mercy, or compassion in him. Satan hates all people. He is the father of lies. He was a liar from the beginning, and he brought sin into our world, using Adam and Eve to disobey God. Read Genesis Chapter 3. Satan was a murderer from the beginning when he enticed Cain to kill his brother Abel through anger. There is no truth in Satan. He hates you and me because we are God's creation and God loves us. Satan hates God and Jesus. Sin separates us from God, but Jesus, being God, died for us on the cross and made it possible for us to come to God through his shedding of His holy blood.

Satan's desire is to keep you away from God and to get you into hell. Read the account of Job in the Old Testament, how a righteous man was persecuted by Satan. Satan uses people to say mean and hurtful things to us. He uses government leaders to pass laws that are not godly, such as gay marriage, abortion, taking prayer and the Bible out of our schools, and taking the Ten Commandments out of our courthouses.

> *Don't you realize that those who do wrong will not inherit the kingdom of God? Don't fool yourselves. Those who indulge in sexual sin, or who worship idols, or commit adultery, or are male prostitutes, or practice homosexuality, or are thieves, or are greedy people, or drunkards, or are abusive, or cheat people—none of these will inherit the Kingdom of God. Some of you were once like that. But you were cleansed; you were made holy; you were made right with God by calling on the name of the Lord Jesus Christ and by the Spirit of our God.*
>
> —*1 CORINTHIANS 6:9-11 (NLT)*

*We know that the law is good when used correctly. For the law was not intended for people who do what is right. It is for people who are lawless and rebellious, who are ungodly and sinful, who consider nothing sacred and defile what is holy, who kill their father or mother or commit other murders. The law is for people who are sexually immoral, or who practice homosexuality, or are slave traders, liars, promise breakers, or who do anything else that contradicts the wholesome teaching that comes from the glorious Good News entrusted to me by our blessed God.*

*—1 TIMOTHY 1:8-11 (NLT)*

Satan is behind adult movies and all pornography, and he preys upon people. Satan likes to blind the eyes and ears of people so they won't believe the Bible and come to Jesus. God's word, the Bible, opens the eyes and ears of people. Demons are evil spirits that want to possess people.

*Then Jesus went to Capernaum, a town in Galilee, and taught there in the synagogue every Sabbath day. There, too, the people were amazed at his teaching, for he spoke with authority.*

*Once when he was in the synagogue, a man possessed by a demon—an evil spirit—began shouting at Jesus, "Go away! Why are you interfering with us, Jesus of Nazareth? Have you come to destroy us? I know who you are—the Holy One of God!"*

*Jesus cut him short. "Be quiet! Come out of the man," he ordered. At that, the demon threw the man to the floor as the crowd watched; then it came out of him without hurting him further.*

*Amazed, the people exclaimed, "What authority and power this man's words possess! Even evil spirits obey him, and they flee at his command!" The news about Jesus spread through every village in the entire region.*

—LUKE 4:31-37 (NLT)

*Now the Holy Spirit tells us clearly that in the last times some will turn away from the true faith; they will follow deceptive spirits and teachings that come from demons. These people are hypocrites and liars, and their consciences are dead.*

—1 TIMOTHY 4:1-2 (NLT

There is only one Lord and worldwide Savior and his name is Jesus. Satan hates Jesus; he was defeated by Jesus on the cross. Jesus doesn't want anyone to go to hell. It was made for Satan and his angels. Jesus is the true door to heaven if we accept him as our savior. His arms are opened to you today, so please take time to accept him as your savior. In the back of this book are words of the sinners' prayer. Say it, believe it, and mean it. Come to Jesus just as you are.

The book of John tells all about who Jesus is. Take time to read John. God will not stop loving you. Don't listen to the evil liar, Satan. You haven't gone over the cliff. It doesn't matter what you have done in the past. JESUS WANTS TO FORGIVE ALL OF YOUR SINS. HIS ARMS ARE OPEN TO ALL WHO ASK FOR FORGIVENESS.

The Bible says that anyone in Christ is a new person. Old things are passed away. You have a new beginning and a fresh start. If you said the sinners' prayer and meant it, all your sins are wiped away and you belong to Christ. Now you belong to the family of God as a son or daughter.

Call God your father. Satan is a liar who will tell you to give up and that you have sinned too much.

> *I, even I, am he who blots out your transgressions, for my own sake, and remembers your sins no more.*
>
> —*ISAIAH 43:25 (NIV)*

Satan will bring up your past mistakes. Say, "Devil they are all under the blood of Jesus."

> *So now there is no condemnation for those who belong to Christ Jesus.*
>
> —*ROMANS 8:1 (NLT)*

God does not hold things on you. The Bible says that there is rejoicing in heaven over one sinner who repents. That sinner may be you. Make heaven happy today. REPENT and ask Jesus to forgive you of your sins. He will.

# Chapter 3
# Satan's Lies

*For you are the children of your father the devil, and you love to do the evil things he does. He was a murderer from the beginning. He has always hated the truth, because there is no truth in him. When he lies, he is consistent with his character; for he is a liar, and the father of lies.*

—JOHN 8:44 (NLT)

Here are some lies that Satan tells people:

**There is no hell.** The truth is, Jesus spoke more about hell than he did about heaven.

> *If your hand causes you to sin, cut it off. It's better to enter eternal life with only one hand than to*

*go into the unquenchable fires of hell with two hands. If your foot causes you to sin, cut it off. It's better to enter eternal life with only one foot than to be thrown into hell with two feet. And if your eye causes you to sin, gouge it out. It's better to enter the Kingdom of God with only one eye than to have two eyes and be thrown into hell, 'where the maggots never die and the fire never goes out.'*

*—MARK 9:43-48 (NLT)*

*Then the devil, who had deceived them, was thrown into the fiery lake of burning sulfur, joining the beast and the false prophet. There they will be tormented day and night forever and ever.*

*—REVELATION 20:10 (NLT)*

There are many more verses listed in the Bible about hell.

***I have never sinned.*** Jesus said that if we say we have no sin, we are calling God a liar. The Bible says we have all sinned and come short of the glory of God.

***I am a good person.*** The Bible says that our righteousness is as filthy as rags and there is none good except God.

***There is no God.*** The Bible says that only fools say that. Even the devil and his demons fear God. Any church that doesn't uplift Jesus as God's only son and savior is false and of the devil.

> *Jesus told him, "I am the way, the truth, and the life. No one can come to the Father except through me."*
>
> *—JOHN 14:6 (NLT)*

***Hell is for Satan only.*** That is a lie. The rich man in the Bible died and went to hell. (Luke 16 v.19-31).

***A loving God wouldn't send people to hell.*** It is our unforgiven sins that send us to hell.

***I am too bad for heaven. I have sinned too much. I'm not good enough.*** The truth is, Jesus died for all sins, and no matter how much bad you have done, Jesus accepts you if you say and mean the prayer of salvation. If you pray that prayer, you will get a brand new start. It's like having a calculator of a high number of sins and then hitting the clear button.

***Everyone goes to heaven, and that is why Jesus died for us.*** The truth is, we must be born again.

Read the story of Nicodemus in the Bible, found in the book of John chapter 3:1-8.

> *For God so loved the world, that he gave his only begotten Son, that whosoever believeth in him should not perish, but have everlasting life.*
>
> *For God sent not his Son into the world to condemn the world; but that the world through him might be saved.*
>
> *He that believeth on him is not condemned; but he that believeth not is condemned already, because he hath not believed in the name of the only begotten Son of God.*
>
> *—JOHN 3:15-18 (KJV)*

***Good people can make it to heaven with or without Christ.*** My aunt believed this lie and told me that she wasn't any worse than anybody else in the world, judging by all the people she knew. She has been in hell for over thirty years and now she knows the truth. My uncle thought he had to quit smoking and drinking before he ever could be born again, and he never did come to Christ. He is dead and now knows the truth of a real hell.

> *Jesus went through the towns and villages, teaching as he went, always pressing on toward Jerusalem. Someone asked him, "Lord, will only a few be saved?"*
>
> *He replied, "Work hard to enter the narrow door to God's Kingdom, for many will try to enter but will fail. When the master of the house has locked the door, it will be too late. You will stand outside knocking and pleading, 'Lord, open the door for us!' But he will reply, 'I don't know you or where you come from.' Then you will say, 'But we ate and drank with you, and you taught in our streets.' And he will reply, 'I tell you, I don't know you or where you come from. Get away from me, all you who do evil.'*
>
> *"There will be weeping and gnashing of teeth, for you will see Abraham, Isaac, Jacob, and all the prophets in the Kingdom of God, but you will be thrown out. And people will come from all over the world—from east and west, north and south—to take their places in the Kingdom of*

*God. And note this: Some who seem least important now will be the greatest then, and some who are the greatest now will be least important then."*

—*LUKE 13:22-30 (NLT)*

**The devil is just a myth.** Satan tempted Jesus and still tempts us. If he gets us to believe he is not real, we will not ever know he is here on Earth to tempt us and destroy us.

*The thief comes only to steal and kill and destroy; I have come that they may have life, and have it to the full.*

—*JOHN 10:10 (NIV)*

*Then Jesus was led by the Spirit into the wilderness to be tempted there by the devil. For forty days and forty nights he fasted and became very hungry.*

*During that time the devil came and said to him, "If you are the Son of God, tell these stones to become loaves of bread."*

*But Jesus told him, "No! The Scriptures say,*

*'People do not live by bread alone, but by every word that comes from the mouth of God.'"*

*Then the devil took him to the holy city, Jerusalem, to the highest point of the Temple, and said, "If you are the Son of God, jump off! For the Scriptures say,*

*'He will order his angels to protect you. And they will hold you up with their hands so you won't even hurt your foot on a stone.'"*

*Jesus responded, "The Scriptures also say, 'You must not test the LORD your God.'"*

*Next the devil took him to the peak of a very high mountain and showed him all the kingdoms of the world and their glory. "I will give it all to you," he said, "if you will kneel down and worship me."*

*"Get out of here, Satan," Jesus told him. "For the Scriptures say,*

*'You must worship the LORD your God and serve only him.'"*

*Then the devil went away, and angels came and took care of Jesus.*

*—MATTHEW 4:1-11 (NLT)*

**I am going to the grave like everyone else; there is no heaven or hell.** Yes, you will go to the grave like everyone else, but after death comes the judgment of God.

> *(For we walk by faith and not by sight:)*
>
> *We are confident, I say, and willing rather to be absent from the body and to be present with the Lord.*
>
> *—2 CORINTHIANS 5:7-8 (KJV)*

No flesh and blood will enter into heaven, only the soul of man which is the real you.

**I will go to heaven because I am a member of a church.** Church won't get you into heaven. Only accepting Jesus and having a relationship with him will get you into heaven.

**The Bible is not to be taken literally, and it is filled with fictional stories.** All scripture is God breathed.

> *All scripture is given by inspiration of God, and is profitable for doctrine, for reproof, for correction, for instruction in righteousness:*
>
> *—2 TIMOTHY 3:16 (KJV)*

Don't wait until you're in hell to find out the truth that the Bible is the written word of God. The Bible is a road map to a relationship with Jesus and eternity in heaven.

***Life ends at death.*** No, it only leads you to eternity, be that heaven or hell. Satan is a liar. He knows the truth. He doesn't want you to read the Bible, nor does he want you to get saved. He hates Jesus and doesn't want you to accept Jesus as your Savior. He wants you to be in hell with him and his demons forever.

> *You can enter God's kingdom only through the narrow gate. The highway to hell is broad, and its gate is wide for the many who choose that way. But the gateway to life is very narrow and the road is difficult, and only a few ever find it.*
>
> *—MATTHEW 7:13-14 (NLT)*

Come to Jesus and you will be on the narrow road.

# Chapter 4
# My Experience in Hell

WARNING!!! No one is scared of hell until he or she gets there. Read Luke Chapter 16 verses 19-31 of the Parable of the Rich Man and Lazarus.

Twice in my life I backslid on God. I mentioned this in Chapter 1. One day my brother Bill came to me and said, "I feel that something is going to happen to you, but I don't know what that will be. One night in 1980 I had no more than lain down and it was like someone turned the lights off on me. I was in total darkness. I said, 'Oh, I must have died.'"

I found myself in tremendous torment. There was a silence there. I felt alone. I wanted to curse God because I knew he created hell and I was in it. In hell there is never a moment of rest.

I was lying on my back in unbelievable evil darkness; I had no strength at all. I thought about my loved ones and wondered if they had my funeral yet. I wondered if my family had died. I did not know how long I had been in hell. There is no time in eternity. Time is only on Earth. In hell you're just there.

I looked up and saw Jesus standing there in a long beige robe with pleats in it. A light shone about him. He appeared to be nearly six feet tall. He had black hair combed straight back and was picture perfect down to his neck. It was not long hair like pictures show him. His hair looked oily like the oil of the Holy Spirit. I never saw his face, because he kept his back to me at all times.

He said to me, "You have backslid on me twice, and you have died and you're in hell."

I was in torment. Bad torment. Hell is evil. I started begging for another chance. He said no. Again, he said, "You have backslid on me twice and are in hell."

I have never experienced fear like I had there. When I talked to Jesus, it was all through thoughts, but they came out as spoken words. As I continued to beg for another chance, Jesus said no and started to walk away. I was so scared that he was going to disappear and leave me there in hell. As he started to walk away, two demonic creatures started to come after me.

They came up from a pit through a tunnel. Your senses are sharp in hell. You know what's happening. These demons had a real hatred for me. I couldn't figure out why they hated me. One was going to bash my face in. I thought, "Why do they hate me?"

I wasn't serving Jesus, but I had been kind and generous and honest to my fellow man. Still, they hated me. I kept begging with increased panic. Jesus stopped and said to me, "I will give you another chance."

I was out of hell faster than a person can snap a finger. THANK YOU, JESUS!!! I would have given everything I ever owned to get out of hell.

I had a friend who dropped dead on a hospital treadmill. They were checking his heart condition, and he died. He was dead for three minutes before the doctors brought him back. He kept telling my stepdad over and over that he never wanted to experience that again. Over and over he said, "I never want to see that again." He didn't want to talk about it.

Because of my experience in hell, I wanted to find out what he experienced in death. When I asked him about it, he kept trying to change the subject. Getting nowhere with him, I told him about my experience in hell. As I started speaking of my experience in hell, he got a stare on his face and his eyes got as big as the moon. He told me that something turned the lights off on him, and it was total black darkness. He told me it was the same thing that I saw, only he did not see Jesus. He was not a Christian.

What I am warning you about is the truth. Hell is a real place. After death comes the judgment of God.

> *And just as each person is destined to die once and after that comes judgment*
>
> *—HEBREWS 9:27 (NLT)*

# Chapter 5
# The Soul, the Real Life of Man

- Life is on the inside of our body. When I was in hell, I was the same person I am now. I had eyes to see, ears to hear, a voice to talk with, and a mind to think. I had all of my emotions. The body is used only to carry us around. It is our physical strength. The soul in hell has no strength. When I was in hell, I couldn't move a finger. I was paralyzed.

The Bible says there was a certain rich man who died and went into hell. He lifted up his eyes (he had eyes to see; he had a tongue that desired water), seeing Abraham. He asked for mercy. There is no mercy in hell. He remembered his brothers. He asked for someone to go back to Earth and warn his brothers of hell. The rich man was in torment. This can be read in the Bible in the book of Luke Chapter 16 verses 19-31. I listed these verses in the last chapter.

We all have known someone—a friend, family member, mother, or father—with whom we enjoyed life. Then death came and we went to his or her funeral. Looking at the body in the casket, we talked, but no answer came. There was no breath and no movement. The life of that person had left the body. The Bible says that God is the God of the living, not the dead. The souls of men never die.

Moses had a physical death. Moses' death is found in the Bible in the book of Deuteronomy Chapter 34 verses 5-9. The Transfiguration Matthew Chapter 17:1-4 mentions Moses, who had died and was there with Jesus. If there was nothing after death, how did Moses appear to Peter along with Jesus? The grave isn't the end of us. NO ONE IS SCARED OF HELL UNTIL THEY GET THERE! Your soul will never die; it's the real you.

I had an Uncle Joe who was married to Aunt Ruth. Aunt Ruth had a sister named Linda, for whom I did a lot. I got mad at Linda and stopped going around her. One night as I began to fall asleep, Uncle Joe appeared to me in my apartment. He looked like a black silhouette or a spirit. He had the shape of a body and said to me, "Lannie, don't be that way to Linda. I am not going to be here. Ruth and Linda are going to need you."

I recognized his voice. He wasn't in a fleshly body as I had known him. He disappeared in front of me. It was a Saturday night. The next day, my sister called me and said, "Did you know Uncle Joe died last night?"

I then remembered he came to my apartment the night before. I thought to myself, *What time was he in my apartment?*

It was between 10:30 p.m. and 11:00 p.m. I asked my sister what time did he die. She answered, "About 10:45 p.m."

Uncle Joe was a Christian who followed the road on Earth leading to heaven. All roads don't lead to heaven. There is no other way.

> *"Enter through the narrow gate. For wide is the gate and broad is the road that leads to destruction, and many enter through it. But small is the gate and narrow the road that leads to life, and only a few find it."*
>
> *—MATTHEW 7:13-14 (NIV)*

You can enter God's kingdom only through the narrow gate. Being saved by Jesus is the entrance to the narrow gate. The highway to hell is broad and its gate is wide for the many who choose to walk that way without Jesus leading them. But the gateway to life is very narrow, the road is difficult, and only a few ever find it.

## The Narrow Door

*Jesus went through the towns and villages, teaching as he went, always pressing on toward Jerusalem. Someone asked him, "Lord, will only a few be saved?" He replied, "Work hard to enter the narrow door to God's Kingdom, for many will try to enter but will fail. When the master of the house has locked the door, it will be too late. You will stand outside knocking and pleading, 'Lord, open the door for us!' But he will reply, 'I don't know you or where you come from.' Then you will say, 'But we ate and drank with you, and you taught in our streets.' And he will reply, 'I tell you, I don't know you or where you come from. Get away from me, all you who do evil.'*

*"There will be weeping and gnashing of teeth, for you will see Abraham, Isaac, Jacob, and all the prophets in the Kingdom of God, but you will be thrown out. And people will come from all over the world—from east and west, north and south—to take their places in the Kingdom of God. And note this: Some who seem least important now will be the greatest then, and some who are the greatest now will be least important then."*

*—LUKE 13:22-30(NLT)*

Saying and not believing in hell does not change the truth. It's a real place: A torture chamber. Some rich people believe they don't need God, but in hell they would give all their riches to God if they could just have another chance in life. If judgment is passed by God, they won't get a second chance. They will be burning alive in a lake of fire.

I read Bill Weise's book about his journey into hell titled, *23 Minutes in Hell*. That is a true account of hell. Get his book and believe it. He told things in his book that I knew only from my experience of going into hell. He spoke of the deep darkness, a pit, a tunnel and two demonic creatures that tormented him and hated him. Remember you will never come to a point of nonexistence, nor will your soul ever die.

> *Then the Lord God formed man from the dust of the ground. He breathed the breath of life into the man's nostrils, and the man became a living person.*

*—GENESIS 2:7 (NLT)*

It's your choice either to have a personal relationship with Jesus and make heaven your home or continue with a life without Jesus. You will die and go be with evil Satan and all his demons and make hell your home for all eternity. Ask Jesus to come into your life now. Pray this prayer and mean it.

> *Dear Jesus,*
>
> *I confess I am a sinner and need you as Lord and Savior. I accept your death on the cross as payment for all my sins. Forgive me for all of my sins. Come into my heart now. I put my trust in you. Take over my life. Amen.*

If you said this prayer and meant it, your name is written down in Jesus' book of life and you've just made heaven your home. Find a good Christian church that preaches Jesus and go as often as you can. Satan will try to stop you from going to church. Satan is your enemy. He is angered at you for accepting Jesus. Get baptized in water.

Don't ever go by feelings. Forget your past sins. Read your Bible. The New Testament is best to read first. The book of John is really good. It tells you about our wonderful Jesus. Praise him and thank him. Jesus loves you.

# Chapter 6
# People

*"Not everyone who says to me, 'Lord, Lord,' shall enter the kingdom of heaven, but he who does the will of My Father in heaven. Many will say to Me in that day, 'Lord, Lord, have we not prophesied in Your name, cast out demons in Your name, and done many wonders in Your name?' And then I will declare to them, 'I never knew you; depart from me, you who practice lawlessness!'*

*"Therefore whoever hears these sayings of Mine, and does them, I will liken him to a wise man who built his house on the rock: and the rain descended, the floods came, and the winds blew*

*and beat on that house; and it did not fall, for it was founded on the rock.*

*"But everyone who hears these sayings of Mine, and does not do them, will be like a foolish man who built his house on the sand: and the rain descended, the floods came, and the winds blew and beat on that house; and it fell. And great was its fall."*

*And so it was, when Jesus had ended these sayings, that the people were astonished at His teaching, for He taught them as one having authority, and not as the scribes.*

*—MATTHEW 7:21-29 (NKJV)*

Not all people who confess God are real Christians. Not all ministers are serving God. Not all churches are pleasing to God. The Bible said that the day will come when people will stand in front of God for judgment. Some were doing works, but didn't have a personal relationship with Jesus. Jesus died for your sins. (John 3:16) Accept his death on the cross for your sins or pay for your own sins. Hell is the payment for your sins, which is total separation from God and heaven.

We are all sinners. It's about God's free grace that he extends to all. Yes, even to you.

> *For by grace are ye saved through faith; and that not of yourself: it is the gift of God:*
>
> *Not of works, least any man should boast.*
>
> *—EPHESIANS 2:8-9 (KJV)*

## Getting Along with People

Not all people in church are easy to be around, but you should learn to love them anyway. Satan will use people to offend you to drive you out of church. Remember, Satan doesn't want you going to a Christian church or growing in a relationship with Jesus.

> *Submit yourselves therefore to God. Resist the devil, and he will flee from you.*
>
> *Draw nigh to God, and he will draw nigh to you. Cleanse your hands, ye sinners; and purify your hearts, ye double minded.*
>
> *—JAMES 4:7-8 (KJV)*

Remember that Satan is mad at those who have accepted Jesus as their savior. REMEMBER TO BE WISE. SATAN, THE DEVIL, IS YOUR ENEMY AND THE DEVIL IS REAL. Don't ever quit!!! Don't ever quit!!! Don't live in your past. The devil will bring your past up to you and try to condemn you or make you feel guilty.

> *Therefore if any man be in Christ, he is a new creature: old things are passed away; behold all things are become new.*
>
> *—2 CORINTHIANS 5:17 (KJV)*

You may still sin or say something bad. (Remember you are like a baby starting out with God.) Just ask God to forgive you and he will. Now forget it and go on with God. God's mercies are new every day for us. We have a brand new start; a new day. Don't ever dwell on your weaknesses. We all have them. Think on the good. Don't look at other people's faults; we all have them. God is still working on you and me, and He is perfecting us to be like Jesus. Don't judge people. God will do that. We are individuals; God made us that way. Love your enemies. Do good to all people.

Be kind and helpful, and become a giver. God made all people worldwide and he loves us all.

Remember that good people do go to hell. Jesus said, "If you deny me, I will deny you before my Father."

> *Whosoever therefore shall confess me before men, him will I confess also before my Father which is in heaven.*
>
> *But whosoever shall deny me before men, him will I also deny before my Father which is in heaven.*
>
> *—MATTHEW 10:32-33 (KJV)*

Don't be ashamed of being a Christian. Honor Jesus with your mouth.

# Chapter 7
# Jesus

Who is Jesus? Jesus is God's Son, and all that God is, Jesus is. Jesus was with God when he created all mankind.

> *And God said, let us make man in our image after our likeness:*
>
> *—GENESIS 1:26a (KJV)*

Jesus was here from the beginning and has always existed. He came to Earth from heaven. His home is in heaven. Why is Jesus the only way into heaven? He is God's Son and he created all of mankind. In fact, everything that is here, Jesus created. He shed his holy blood for the sins of the whole world: Yours and mine.

> *For God so loved the world, that he gave his only begotten Son, that whosoever believeth in him should not perish, but have everlasting life.*
>
> *For God sent not his Son into the world to condemn the world; but that the world through him might be saved.*
>
> *He that believeth on him is not condemned: but he that believeth not is condemned already, because he hath not believed in the name of the only begotten Son of God.*
>
> —JOHN 3:16-18 (KJV)

I thought one day of all the things Jesus has done—not the things he has done just for others, but for me as well. I said, "Jesus, what can I do to repay you for all you've done for me?"

I said, "I can't buy you a car because you won't drive it. I can't bake you a cake because you won't eat it. What can I do for you, Jesus?"

He spoke to me and said, "Feed my sheep."

God wants us to help and give and care for all born-again Christians.

> *The father loveth the Son, and hath given all things into his hand.*
>
> *He that believeth on the Son hath everlasting life: and he that believeth not the Son shall not see life; but the wrath of God abideth on him.*
>
> —*JOHN 3:35-36 (KJV)*
>
> *And Jesus came and spake unto them, saying, All power is given unto me in heaven and in earth.*
>
> *Go ye therefore, and teach all nations, baptizing them in the name of the Father, and of the Son, and of the Holy Ghost:*
>
> *Teaching them to observe all things whatsoever I have commanded you: and, lo, I am with you always, even unto the end of the world. Amen.*
>
> —*MATTHEW 28:18-20 (KJV)*

> *(Jesus said) I am he that liveth and was dead; and behold, I am alive forever more, Amen; and have the keys of hell and death.*
>
> *—REVELATION 28:18-20 (KJV)*

Jesus has the power over Satan and demons. Jesus is the King of kings and Lord of lords. Jesus is ahead of all and is everything.

> *For all have sinned, and come short of the glory of God.*
>
> *—ROMANS 3:23 (KJV)*

> *So then, since we have a great High Priest who has entered heaven, Jesus the Son of God, let us hold firmly to what we believe. This High Priest of ours understands our weaknesses, for he faced all of the same testings we do, yet he did not sin. So let us come boldly to the throne of our gracious God. There we will receive his mercy, and we will find grace to help us when we need it most.*
>
> *—HEBREWS 4:14-16 (NLT)*

This high priest of ours understands our weaknesses, for he faced all of the same testings we do, yet he did not sin.

Jesus is a wonderful Lord and Savior; he really loves you. Read the whole book of John in the Bible. Go to the New Testament and you will find it after the book of Luke. Make Jesus your best friend by asking him into your heart and life. Jesus will be your best friend you will ever have.

# Chapter 8
# Born Again (Saved)

Jesus told Nicodemus, "You must be born again."

This only comes about by believing and trusting Jesus for your new life. You can trust Jesus by asking Him to forgive you for all of your sins and accepting his forgiveness. Forgiveness comes through the shedding of his holy blood on the cross of Calvary. Make Jesus the Lord of your total life, and you will receive the Holy Spirit and will be born again.

> *There was a man named Nicodemus, a Jewish religious leader who was a Pharisee. After dark one*

*evening, he came to speak with Jesus. "Rabbi," he said, "we all know that God has sent you to teach us. Your miraculous signs are evidence that God is with you."*

*Jesus replied, "I tell you the truth, unless you are born again, you cannot see the Kingdom of God."*

*"What do you mean?" exclaimed Nicodemus. "How can an old man go back into his mother's womb and be born again?"*

*Jesus replied, "I assure you, no one can enter the Kingdom of God without being born of water and the Spirit. Humans can reproduce only human life, but the Holy Spirit gives birth to spiritual life. So don't be surprised when I say, 'You must be born again'. The wind blows wherever it wants. Just as you can hear the wind but can't tell where it comes from or where it is going, so you can't explain how people are born of the Spirit."*

*"How are these things possible?" Nicodemus asked.*

*Jesus replied, "You are a respected Jewish teacher, and yet you don't understand these things? I assure you, we tell you what we know and have seen, and yet you won't believe our testimony. But if you don't believe me when I tell you about earthly things, how can you possibly believe if I tell you about heavenly things? No one has ever gone to heaven and returned. But the Son of Man has come down from heaven. And as Moses lifted up the bronze snake on a pole in the wilderness, so the Son of Man must be lifted up, so that everyone who believes in him will have eternal life.*

*—JOHN 3:1-15 (NLT)*

Praise Jesus that anything you or I have ever done—murder, lying, stealing, adultery, cursing, abortion, and all other sins—are forgiven and never to be remembered by God again when we accept Jesus as our Lord and Savior. Jesus is alive and well today. He is for you and not against you. He is a true friend. Cast all your cares on Jesus. Yes, all of them, for he cares for you. For Jesus sits on the throne of Heaven, and he has all the answers you need.

You now have a new start in life. Jesus has paid the price for the whole world. He is the world's only hope. We must be born again through Jesus.

If you have accepted Jesus, his blood has cleansed you from all sins as a free gift. God gives us his free gift. Grace is a free gift to all mankind. It's not by your good works; it's only by what Jesus has already done for you and me.

THANK YOU, JESUS!!!

# Chapter 9
# Deceiving Sins

Satan wants you to believe false statements and have many people be deceived. The Bible tells us the truth. In this chapter we will cover false statements and the truth to give you knowledge so you are not deceived.

## THE DECEPTION

"I'm going to heaven because I go to church every week and put money in the offering plate."

"I am a good person."

"I belong to a Catholic church and I am a member, so I know I am going to heaven. All members of our church are going to heaven."

"Our denomination is God's chosen; we are the only true church."

## THE TRUTH

Heaven is ours only through Jesus Christ. Joining a church or denomination will not save you; you must be born again.

> *As it is written, there is none righteous, no, not one:*
>
> *There is none that understandeth, there is none that seeketh after God.*
>
> *They are all gone out of the way, they are together become unprofitable; there is none that doeth good, no, not one.*
>
> *—ROMANS 3:10-12 (KJV)*

## THE DECEPTION

"I don't sin; I only have faults."

"I am gay and I was born that way."

## THE TRUTH

We are all born sinners but we are not to stay that way. That is why Christ died for us. We must be born again. Anyone who thinks they don't sin and only have faults will believe they have no need for a Savior. No one who practices a life of sin will enter into the kingdom of Heaven. Jesus is the only way we can be cleansed of our sins.

## THE DECEPTION

"It is okay to have an open marriage because we both agree to have sex with other people. It doesn't hurt anyone."

## THE TRUTH

God did not make our bodies to lust (or desire) after. God hates sexual sins.

> *You must not commit adultery.*
>
> *—EXODUS 20:14 (NLT)*

> *And Jesus replied: "You must not murder. You must not commit adultery. You must not steal. You must not testify falsely."*
>
> *—MATTHEW 19:18b (NLT)*

> *You have heard the commandments that say, "You must not commit adultery." But I say, anyone who even looks at a woman with lust has already committed adultery with her in his heart.*
>
> *—MATTHEW 5:27-27 (NLT)*

## THE DECEPTION

"I have sinned way too much to be saved. God would never forgive me. You don't know all the bad that I have done."

## THE TRUTH

No one who calls on the name of the Lord and means it will be refused, no matter how much sin or wrong they have done. NO ONE IS REJECTED!!!

> *But everyone who calls on the name of the Lord will be saved.*
>
> *—ACTS 2:21 (NLT)*

## THE DECEPTION

"I don't have to go to church. I can stay home and get all I need."

## THE TRUTH

We draw strength and encouragement from one another. Iron sharpens iron.

*And let us not neglect our meeting together, as some people do, but encourage one another, especially now that the day of His return is drawing near.*

*—HEBREWS 10:25(NLT)*

## THE DECEPTION

"Hell is only for the devil and his angels. People don't go there."

## THE TRUTH

Read the verses below, paying close attention to verses 24 -27.

> *[19]Jesus said, "There was a certain rich man who was splendidly clothed in purple and fine linen and who lived each day in luxury. [20]At his gate lay a poor man named Lazarus who was covered with sores. [21]As Lazarus lay there longing for scraps from the rich man's table, the dogs would come and lick his open sores.*
>
> *[22]"Finally, the poor man died and was carried by the angels to be with Abraham. The rich man al-*

*so died and was buried, ²³ and his soul went to the place of the dead. There, in torment, he saw Abraham in the far distance with Lazarus at his side.*

*²⁴ "The rich man shouted, 'Father Abraham, have some pity! Send Lazarus over here to dip the tip of his finger in water and cool my tongue. I am in anguish in these flames.'*

*²⁵ "But Abraham said to him, 'Son, remember that during your lifetime you had everything you wanted, and Lazarus had nothing. So now he is here being comforted, and you are in anguish. ²⁶ And besides, there is a great chasm separating us. No one can cross over to you from here, and no one can cross over to us from there.'*

*²⁷ "Then the rich man said, 'Please, Father Abraham, at least send him to my father's home. ²⁸ For I have five brothers, and I want him to warn them so they don't end up in this place of torment.'*

*²⁹ "But Abraham said, 'Moses and the prophets have warned them. Your brothers can read what they wrote.'*

> *[30] "The rich man replied, 'No, Father Abraham! But if someone is sent to them from the dead, then they will repent of their sins and turn to God.'*
>
> *[31] "But Abraham said, 'If they won't listen to Moses and the prophets, they won't listen even if someone rises from the dead.*
>
> —LUKE 16:19-31(NLT)

You will go to hell if you reject the son of God. Jesus is his name. Satan is the father of lies. There is no truth in him. He is the master deceiver of the whole world.

# Chapter 10
# Love

*If I could speak all the languages of earth and of angels, but didn't love others, I would only be a noisy gong or a clanging cymbal. If I had the gift of prophecy, and if I understood all of God's secret plans and possessed all knowledge, and if I had such faith that I could move mountains, but didn't love others, I would be nothing. If I gave everything I have to the poor and even sacrificed my body, I could boast about it; but if I didn't love others, I would have gained nothing.*

*Love is patient and kind. Love is not jealous or boastful or proud or rude. It does not demand its own way. It is not irritable, and it keeps no record of being wronged. It does not rejoice about injustice but rejoices whenever the truth wins out. Love never gives up, never loses faith, is always hopeful, and endures through every circumstance.*

*Prophecy and speaking in unknown languages and special knowledge will become useless. But love will last forever! Now our knowledge is partial and incomplete, and even the gift of prophecy reveals only part of the whole picture! But when the time of perfection comes, these partial things will become useless.*

*When I was a child, I spoke and thought and reasoned as a child. But when I grew up, I put away childish things. Now we see things imperfectly, like puzzling reflections in a mirror, but then we will see everything with perfect clarity. All that I know now is partial and incomplete, but then I will know everything completely, just as God now knows me completely.*

*Three things will last forever—faith, hope, and love—and the greatest of these is love.*

*—1 CORINTHIANS 13 (NLT)*

All good we do to help others pleases God. God is love. Love the sinner but hate the sin. Love does not keep a record of wrong. When you or I forgive others of their sins and hurts against us, we free ourselves by letting go of past offenses. We are free to move on past that area of our life. God forgives you and me when we ask him to. We need to forgive even when they don't ask us to be forgiven, and even when they're not sorry. Because of His love for you and me, Jesus went to the cross and shed his blood for the sins of the whole world.

> *For God loved the world so much that he gave his one and only son, so that everyone who believes in him will not perish but have eternal life.*
>
> *—JOHN 3:16 (NLT)*

Remember if you come to Jesus he will never reject or turn you away. God loves you.

## **THE PRAYER FOR SALVATION**

*Jesus,*

*I confess my sins. I am a sinner and need a Savior. I believe you died on the cross for me. Forgive me of all my sins and wash me clean. Come into my heart and be lord of my life. Amen.*

## Salvation

1. John 3:3-6  We must be born again
2. 2 Corinthians 5:17-21  We become new creatures
3. Romans 10: 9-10  How to receive
4. Acts 2:21  Whoever calls on him will be saved
5. John 3:16-18  God so loved the world he gave his son
6. Ephesians 2:8  Salvation is a free gift
7. Revelation 3:20  God knocks

If you said this prayer and meant it, you are now born again. Get water baptized. Read the Bible daily. Go to a Christian church where Jesus is preached and honored as Lord. Love God and love others. God loves you—yes, you—just as you are.

If you would like to contact me for speaking engagements or this book has blessed you, my g-mail address is:

r.lannie47@gmail.com

# The Fresh Ink Group

Publishing
Free Memberships
Free Stories, Essays, Articles
Free-Story Newsletter
Writing Contests

Books
E-books
Amazon Bookstore

Authors
Editors
Artists
Professionals
Publishing Services
Publisher Resources

Readers' Forum
Blogs
Social Media

www.FreshInkGroup.com

Email: info@FreshInkGroup.com

**The Fresh Ink Group is a proud member of
The Coalition of Independent Authors and Publishers**

www.ingramcontent.com/pod-product-compliance
Lightning Source LLC
Chambersburg PA
CBHW060505080526
44584CB00015B/1551